Steck-Vaughn
Real-Life English
GRAMMAR

Book 1

Richard Firsten
ESOL and Adult Literacy Instructor
Dade County Public Schools

Reviewers

Fiona Armstrong
ESOL Specialist
New York City Adult Basic Education

Anne Ediger
Curriculum Coordinator
American Language Institute
San Diego State University

Ed Schiffer
ESOL Instructor/Chairperson
Fienberg/Fisher Adult and
Community Education Center
Miami, Florida

STECK-VAUGHN
COMPANY
ELEMENTARY • SECONDARY • ADULT • LIBRARY

Acknowledgments

Richard Firsten has been teaching English as a Second Language since 1969. He is currently an ESOL and Literacy instructor at Lindsey Hopkins Technical Education Center in Miami. Mr. Firsten has taught ESOL methodology at the University of Miami, Nova University in Ft. Lauderdale, Florida International University in Miami, and Florida Atlantic University in Boca Raton.

Illustration

Gary McElhaney
Larry Raymond

Staff Credits

Supervising Editor: Carolyn M. Hall
Senior Editor: Beverly A. Grossman
Cover Design: James Masch
Cover Photography: © Rohan/TSW-CLICK/Chicago

ISBN 0-8114-4625-5

5 6 7 8 9 0 PO 96 95

Contents

Unit 1

☐ **Persons and things**
☐ **Be**
☐ **My, your, his, her...**

Persons and things

Persons: Use **I, you, he, she, we, they.**

I am a student.

You are a student.

You and **I** are students.
We are students.

Sylvia is a student.
She is a student.

Juan is a student.
He is a student.

Sylvia and Juan are students.
They are students.

Things: Use **it, they.**   **It** is a book.   **They** are books.

Fill in the blanks.

1. Fidel is a student. ____He____ lives in Miami.

2. My name is Maria. _____ am from Mexico.

3. Hello, Steve. How are _____?

4. Mark and Lisa are students. _____ are in high school.

5. I like English. _____ is interesting.

6. Mark and I are in this class. _____ are friends.

7. Ms. Smith is the teacher. _____ is a good teacher.

Be

Long form:				Short form:	
I	**am**	we	**are**	I**'m**	we**'re**
you	**are**			you**'re**	
he	**is**			he**'s**	
she	**is**	they	**are**	she**'s**	they**'re**
it	**is**			it**'s**	

A. Fill in the blanks. Use the long form.

1. You ___are___ from Mexico.

2. Ivan _____ from the Soviet Union.

3. Marie and Paul _____ from Canada.

4. We _____ friends.

5. He _____ the teacher.

B. Fill in the blanks. Use the short form.

1. They are in this class. ___They're___ in this class.

2. We are English students. _____ English students.

3. She is from France. _____ from France.

4. You are my friend. _____ my friend.

5. I am an English student. _____ an English student.

6. It is cold in Minnesota. _____ cold in Minnesota.

7. He is my teacher. _____ my teacher.

8. We are friends. _____ friends.

9. I am from El Salvador. _____ from El Salvador.

10. It is nice to meet you. _____ nice to meet you.

Be: Negatives

Long form:	Short form:
I am **not**	I'm **not**
You are **not**	You aren't
He is **not**	He isn't
She is **not**	She isn't
It is **not**	It isn't
We are **not**	We aren't
They are **not**	They aren't

Fill in the blanks. Use the short form.

1. Maria is Italian. She ___isn't___ American.

2. Fidel is from Miami. He _____ from New York.

3. I am Binh. I _____ Kai.

4. Mark and Lisa are students. They _____ teachers.

5. It is cold in Minnesota. It _____ hot.

6. You're the English teacher. You _____ the math teacher.

7. My zip code is 78412. It _____ 78413.

8. You are young. You _____ old.

9. We are happy today. We _____ sad.

10. He is a man. He _____ a boy.

11. She is at home. She _____ at school.

12. Her first name is Sonia. It _____ Sarah.

13. Emma and Paul are French. They _____ German.

14. I am nineteen. I _____ twenty-one.

15. Your teacher is from San Diego. She _____ from Irvine.

Be: Questions and answers

Am I late?   Yes, I am.

Am	I	late?	Yes,	I am.	*or*	No,	I'm not.
Are	you			you are.			you aren't.
Is	he			he is.			he isn't.
Is	she			she is.			she isn't.
Is	it			it is.			it isn't.
Are	we			we are.			we aren't.
Are	they			they are.			they aren't.

A. Answer the questions.

1. Is Jack American? Yes, _____ he is _____.

2. Is it cold in Minnesota? Yes, _____.

3. Are we late? No, _____.

4. Is Maria Mexican? Yes, _____.

5. Is Minnesota a state? Yes, _____.

6. Are California and Texas states? Yes, _____.

B. Work with a classmate. Ask each other these questions.

1. Are you happy?

2. Are you a student?

3. Are you American?

My, your, his, her . . .

These words say a person <u>has</u> something.

I have **my** book.   You have **your** book.

He has **his** book.
She has **her** book.
We have **our** books.
They have **their** books.

Fill in the blanks. Use **my, your, his, her, our,** and **their.**

1. Hello. ___My___ name is Juan.

2. I have a sister. _____ name is Berta.

3. I have a brother. _____ name is Carlos.

4. We live in Miami. _____ address is 23 Elm Street.

5. Jack and Steve are brothers. _____ parents live in Chicago.

6. We are in English class. Mr. Smith is _____ teacher.

7. Mr. and Mrs. Abrams are from Texas. _____ home is in Houston.

8. You are in math class. Ms. Jones is _____ teacher.

9. Maria lives in San Diego. _____ area code is 619.

10. It's nice to meet you. What is _____ name?

Write It! Say It! Do It!

A. Ask a classmate these questions.

1. What is your name?

2. What is your address?

3. What city do you live in?

4. What state do you live in?

5. What is your zip code?

6. What is your telephone number?

7. What is your nationality?

8. What is your social security number?

B. Now fill in the form. Give your own information.

Name: _____

       Last   First   Middle

Address: _____

       Number and Street

       _____

       City   State   Zip Code

Phone: **(home)** _____   _____

                Area Code   Phone Number

         (work) _____   _____

                Area Code   Phone Number

Nationality: _____

Social Security Number: _____ - _____ - _____

Unit 2

☐ **A *or* an**
☐ **Who? What? Where? How far?**
☐ **Right now**

A *or* an

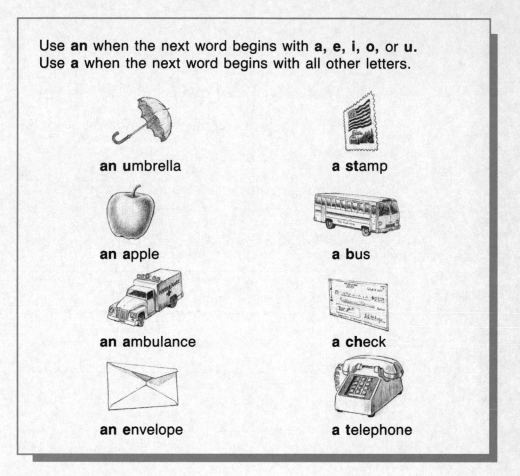

Use **an** when the next word begins with **a, e, i, o,** or **u.**
Use **a** when the next word begins with all other letters.

an umbrella   **a st**amp

an apple   **a b**us

an ambulance   **a ch**eck

an envelope   **a t**elephone

Fill in the blanks with a or an.

1. My sister works at __*a*__ dental clinic on Main Street.

2. I go to _____ barbershop for _____ haircut.

3. I can buy _____ orange and _____ banana in _____ supermarket.

4. If it's _____ emergency, call 911.

5. _____ hospital has _____ ambulance.

6. _____ art museum is _____ place to see paintings.

Who? What? Where? How far?

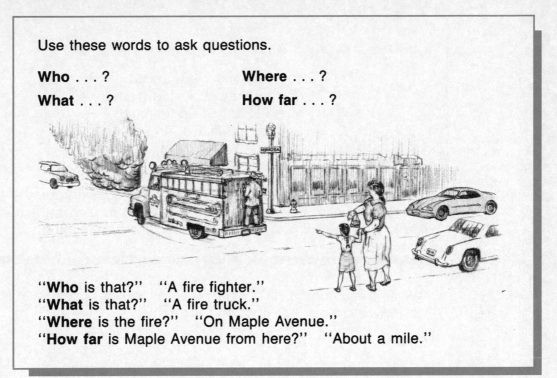

Use these words to ask questions.

Who . . . ?   **Where** . . . ?

What . . . ?   **How far** . . . ?

"**Who** is that?"   "A fire fighter."
"**What** is that?"   "A fire truck."
"**Where** is the fire?"   "On Maple Avenue."
"**How far** is Maple Avenue from here?"   "About a mile."

A. **Fill in the blanks. Use Who, What, Where, and How far to ask questions.**

1. " _Where_ is the fire truck now?" "On Mimosa Street."

2. "_____ is Mimosa Street from Maple Avenue?" "Just two blocks."

3. "_____ is on the fire truck?" "The fire fighter."

4. "_____ is his name?" "Mr. Parker."

B. **Work with a classmate. Ask each other these questions.**

1. **Who** is your best friend?

2. **What** is her (his) phone number?

3. **Where** is she (he) from?

4. **How far** is her (his) home from here?

Right now

Use a form of **be** + verb + **-ing** to show action *right now.*

> I **am** eat + **-ing** dinner.
> You **are** eat + **-ing** dinner.
> He **is** eat + **-ing** dinner.
> They **are** eat + **-ing** dinner.

Long form:

I am speak**ing** on the phone.
You **are** read**ing** this sentence.
He **is** wash**ing** his car.

Short form:

→ **I'm** speak**ing** on the phone.
→ You**'re** read**ing** this sentence.
→ He**'s** wash**ing** his car.

A. What is happening right now? Use the words mailing, catching, using, reading. Use the long form.

1. _____ They are catching _____ a bus.

2. _____ the telephone.

3. _____ a letter.

4. _____ a newspaper.

B. Write about what you are doing right now. Use the words sitting, completing, and studying.

1. _____ I am sitting _____ in the classroom.

2. _____ this sentence.

3. _____ English.

Right now: Negatives

Use a form of **be** + **not** + verb + **-ing** to make the negative.

Long form: Short form:

I **am not** wait**ing** for a taxi.   →   I'm **not** wait**ing** for a taxi.
She **is not** go**ing** to the clinic.   →   She **isn't** go**ing** to the clinic.
They **are not** cash**ing** checks.   →   They **aren't** cash**ing** checks.

Make these sentences negative. Use the short form.

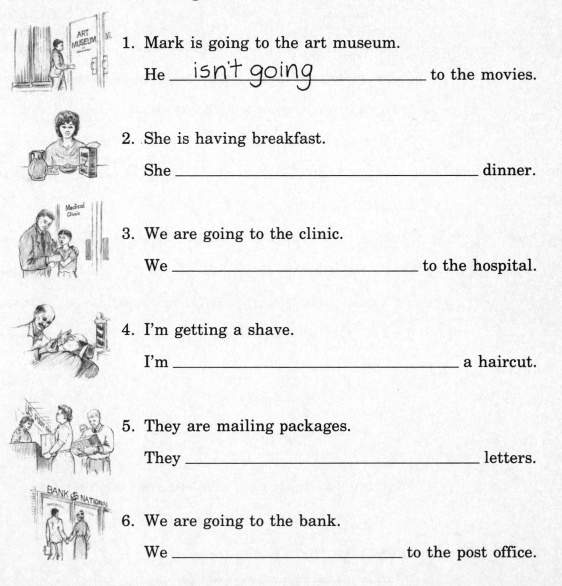

1. Mark is going to the art museum.

   He ___isn't going___ to the movies.

2. She is having breakfast.

   She _____ dinner.

3. We are going to the clinic.

   We _____ to the hospital.

4. I'm getting a shave.

   I'm _____ a haircut.

5. They are mailing packages.

   They _____ letters.

6. We are going to the bank.

   We _____ to the post office.

Right now: Questions and short answers

Questions: Answers:

Is he   playing?   Yes, **he is.**   No, **he isn't.**

Are you   Yes, **I am.**   No, **I'm not.**
Are we   Yes, **we are.**   No, **we aren't.**
Are they   Yes, **they are.**   No, **they aren't.**

A. Change these sentences into questions.

1. They are calling 911.

   _Are they calling 911_____?

2. She is getting a money order.

   _____?

3. Steve is catching the bus.

   _____?

4. You are waiting in line.

   _____?

5. I am disturbing you.

   _____?

B. What are you doing *right now*? Answer the questions.

1. Are you sitting in class? _Yes, I am_____.

2. Are you writing? _____.

3. Are you getting a haircut? _____.

Write It! Say It! Do It!

A. Look at the picture. What is happening? Write the correct letters to complete the sentences.

_____ 1. The children   a. is jumping up and down.

_____ 2. The taxi driver   b. is shaking his fist.

_____ 3. The farmer   c. is directing traffic.

_____ 4. The chickens   d. are running away.

_____ 5. The policewoman   e. are chasing the chickens.

B. Look at the picture again. Make your own questions and answers.

1. Is the policewoman _chasing the chickens_ ?
   No, she isn't .

2. Are the children _____?
   _____.

3. Is the farmer _____?
   _____.

4. Are the chickens _____?
   _____.

5. Is the taxi driver _____?
   _____.

This/that

This = a person or thing *near* you (here).

This is a pencil.

This pencil is sharp.

This is Mrs. Diaz.

This woman is our principal.

That = a person or thing *far* from you (there).

That is our math book.

That book is difficult.

That is Mr. Williams.

That man is our counselor.

Fill in the blanks with **this** or **that**.

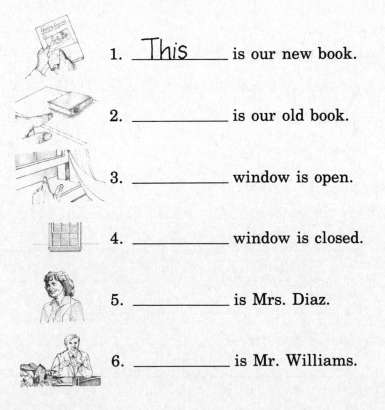

1. __This__ is our new book.

2. _____ is our old book.

3. _____ window is open.

4. _____ window is closed.

5. _____ is Mrs. Diaz.

6. _____ is Mr. Williams.

These/those

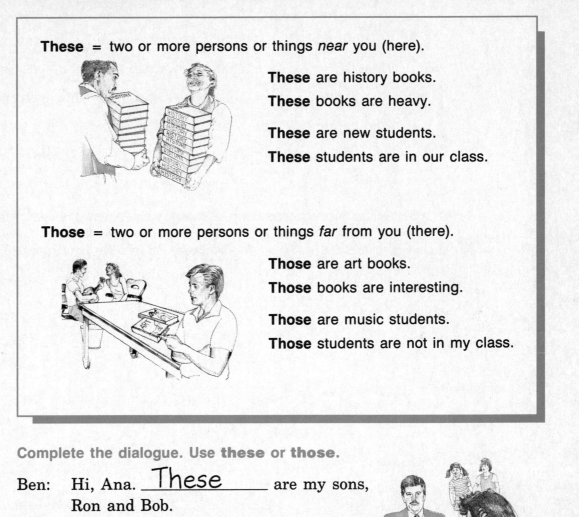

These = two or more persons or things *near* you (here).

These are history books.
These books are heavy.

These are new students.
These students are in our class.

Those = two or more persons or things *far* from you (there).

Those are art books.
Those books are interesting.

Those are music students.
Those students are not in my class.

Complete the dialogue. Use **these** or **those**.

Ben: Hi, Ana. ___These___ are my sons, Ron and Bob.

Ana: And who are _____ girls over there?

Ben: _____ are my daughters, Sue and Ellen.

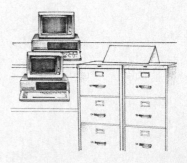

Beto: This is the school library.

Alma: What are _____?

Beto: They're file cabinets.

Alma: And what are _____ machines over there?

Beto: _____ are computers.

Questions and answers

What is **this**?	**This** is a computer.	*or* It's a computer.
What is **that**?	**That**'s a videodisc.	*or* It's a videodisc.
Who is **this**?	**This** is my sister.	*or* It's my sister.
Who is **that**?	**That**'s my teacher.	*or* It's my teacher.
What are **these**?	**These** are crayons.	*or* They're crayons.
What are **those**?	**Those** are erasers.	*or* They're erasers.

Look at the picture. Read the answer. Then write the question.

1. _____What is this_____?
It's a ruler.

2. _____?
It's my daughter.

3. _____?
That's the cafeteria.

4. _____?
These are violins.

5. _____?
Those are enrollment forms.

6. _____?
That's our secretary.

Right now

A. Today is enrollment day at Jefferson Elementary School. Look at the picture. Then choose words from the box to fill in the blanks below.

| standing | making | enrolling | smiling | holding | talking |

These parents are _enrolling_ their children in school. They are _____ in line. The secretary is _____ to a mother. The little girl is _____ a new friend. The children are _____ hands and _____.

B. Look at the picture again. Answer the questions. Use short answers.

1. Are parents enrolling their children?

   Yes, they are.

2. Is the secretary talking to a child?

   _____.

3. Is the mother playing?

   _____.

4. Is the little girl making a new friend?

   _____.

5. Are the children holding hands?

   _____.

In, on, near

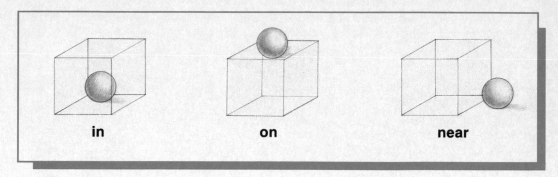

in   on   near

Fill in the blanks with in, on, or near. Use the picture to help you.

1. The book is __on__ the table.

2. The teacher is _____ the door.

3. The wastebasket is _____ the table.

4. The pencil is _____ the floor.

5. The plant is _____ the window.

6. The chalk is _____ the box.

7. The flag is _____ the chalkboard.

8. The teacher is _____ the classroom.

9. The pencils are _____ the cup.

10. The cup is _____ the table.

Write It! Say It! Do It!

A. **What is happening right now? Answer the questions.**

1. What is the teacher doing right now?

   _____.

2. What are you doing right now?

   _____.

3. What book are you using?

   _____.

4. Is your best friend working today?

   _____.

5. What is he/she doing?

   _____.

6. Who is sitting near you?

   _____.

B. **Interview a classmate. Ask each other these questions. Write the answers. Use in, on, or near.**

1. Where is your pencil?

   _____.

2. Where is your English book?

   _____.

3. Where is the teacher?

   _____.

4. Where are you sitting?

   _____.

5. Where are your keys?

   _____.

6. Where is your money?

   _____.

It's usual

Some actions happen again and again. These are *usual* actions.

I   **work** hard every day.
You
We
They

With *he*, *she*, or *it*, add -s or -es.

He   **works** hard every day.   **He**   **goes** to the beach every summer.

Fill in the blanks. Use words from the box below.

works	catches	eats	sleeps	goes	begins	reads

My father ___works___ at night. He _____ during the day. Most people begin work at 8 A.M., but Dad _____ his day at 8 P.M.! He _____ the bus at 7 P.M. He _____ from 8:00 P.M. to 4:00 A.M. Then he comes home. He _____ the newspaper and _____ a bowl of cereal. The family gets up—and he _____ to bed!

It's usual: Negatives

To make the negative, use **don't** with *I, you, we,* and *they.*

Добрый вечер!

Good evening!

I   speak Russian.
You
We
They

I   **don't** speak Russian.
You
We
They

Use **doesn't** with *he, she,* and *it.*

He   likes ice cream.
She

He   **doesn't** like broccoli.
She

A. Write about yourself.

I speak _____, but I don't speak _____.

I enjoy _____, but I don't enjoy

_____. I like _____ weather,

but I don't like _____ weather. I eat

_____, but I don't eat _____.

B. Describe a friend. Fill in the first blank with his/her name.

_____ speaks _____, but

he/she doesn't speak _____. _____

likes _____ weather, but _____

_____ like _____ weather.

It's usual: Questions and answers

With *I, you, we,* or *they,* use **do** and **don't.**

Do you speak Spanish?　　　　Yes, **I**　　**do.**　*or*　No, **I**　　**don't.**
　　we　　　　　　　　　　　　　　　we　　　*or*　　we
　　they　　　　　　　　　　　　　　they　　*or*　　they

A. Answer the questions.

1. Do you get up early? _____.

2. Do you take the bus to class? _____.

3. Do you work on Saturdays? _____.

4. Do you eat lunch at home? _____.

5. Do you like cold weather? _____.

6. Do you like the beach? _____.

7. Do you live in an apartment? _____.

With *he, she,* and *it,* use **does** or **doesn't.**

Does she like ice cream?　　Yes, **she does.**　*or*　No, **she doesn't.**
　　he　　　　　　　　　　　　　　he　　　　*or*　　he

B. Answer the questions.

1. Does your teacher speak Spanish? _____.

2. Does your teacher eat fish? _____.

3. Does your teacher watch TV? _____.

4. Does your teacher like cold weather? _____.

5. Does your teacher like the beach? _____.

6. Does your teacher get up early? _____.

How often?

How often do you eat breakfast?   Every morning.
               read a newspaper?   Every evening.
               brush your teeth?   Three times a day.

How often does he   go to the dentist?   Twice a year.
               she pay the bills?   Once a month.

A. Answer the questions.

1. How often do you study English? _____

    _____.

2. How often do you go to the movies? _____

    _____.

3. How often do you watch TV? _____

    _____.

4. How often do you eat fish? _____

    _____.

5. How often do you ride a bus? _____

    _____.

B. Ask a classmate the questions in Exercise A.
Then write complete sentences about your classmate.

1. _____ studies English _____.

2. He/she _____.

3. _____.

4. _____.

5. _____.

Command/suggest

Commands:

Keep America beautiful.   **Throw** trash here.

Don't walk on the grass.   **Don't litter.**

A. A child and his mother are talking. Match what they say. Write the letters.

Child	Mother
_C_ 1. I have nothing to do.	a. Eat your lunch.
____ 2. I'm hungry.	b. Put on your raincoat.
____ 3. This sandwich is terrible.	c. Go outside and play.
____ 4. It's raining.	d. Go to bed.
____ 5. I'm sleepy.	e. Don't eat it.

Suggestions:
Let's go to the lake this weekend. **Let's not stay** home.

B. Make suggestions (for yourself and others).

1. The TV is broken. _____.

2. We're hungry. _____.

3. It's Saturday night. _____.

4. It's the 4th of July. _____.

5. It's my birthday. _____.

C. Make suggestions (for yourself and others) **not** to do something.

1. I'm tired. _____.

2. It's cold and rainy. _____.

3. The water is polluted. _____.

Write It! Say It! Do It!

A. Write about Jackie. Fill in the blanks. Use words from the box.

studies	takes	works	goes

1. On Tuesday and Thursday, Jackie _goes_ to nursing school.

2. Every Monday, Wednesday, and Friday, she _____ English.

3. She _____ at a restaurant on weekends.

4. Every summer, she _____ a vacation.

B. How often does Jackie do these things? Fill in the blanks.

1. Jackie goes to nursing school _twice a week_____.

2. She studies English _____.

3. She works at a restaurant _____.

4. She takes a vacation _____.

C. Write about your native country.

1. In the summer, people in my country _____

_____.

2. In the afternoon, people _____

_____.

3. People in my country like _____.

They don't like _____.

- □ **Plurals**
- □ **Much/many**
- □ **Whose?/mine, yours**
- □ **Always . . . never**

Plurals

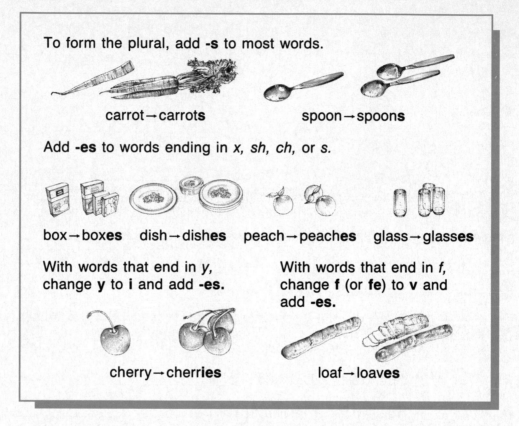

To form the plural, add **-s** to most words.

carrot→carrot**s**   spoon→spoon**s**

Add **-es** to words ending in *x, sh, ch,* or *s.*

box→box**es**   dish→dish**es**   peach→peach**es**   glass→glass**es**

With words that end in *y,* change **y** to **i** and add **-es.**

With words that end in *f,* change **f** (or **fe**) to **v** and add **-es.**

cherry→cherr**ies**   loaf→loa**ves**

Use words in the box below. Write the plural form below.

| grape | radish | knife | glass | fork | strawberry |

1. <u>forks</u>

2. _____

3. _____

4. _____

5. _____

6. _____

Plurals: Things we count

Here are some things we count—

apples   eggs   cookies   onions   oranges

Here are some things we *don't* count—

water   milk   sugar   bread   soup   cheese

except in certain ways:

a **bottle** of water   3 **cups** of sugar   4 **cans** of soup

2 **glasses** of milk   a **piece** of cheese   a **loaf** of bread

Look at the picture. What is on the shelves?

1.   3 cans of milk   2. _____

3. _____   4. _____

5. _____   6. _____

7. _____   8. _____

9. _____   10. _____

Much/many

How **much** milk do we have?   Not **much.**
How **many** apples do we have?   Not **many.**

A. **Luis and Lupe are camping out. They are making a shopping list.
Complete the dialogue with much or many.**

Lupe: How __much__ bread do we have?

Luis: Not _____. Only one loaf.

Lupe: How _____ water do we have?
Luis: Two bottles.

Lupe: How _____ apples do we have?

Luis: Not _____. Just two.

Lupe: How _____ onions do we have?
Luis: A lot. We don't need onions.

B. **What do you eat and drink? Fill in the blanks.**

1. How _____ eggs do you eat every week? _____

2. How _____ water do you drink every day?

    _____

3. How _____ cups of coffee do you drink every day?

    _____

4. How _____ pieces of fruit do you eat every day?

    _____

Whose?/mine, yours . . .

Whose is this?	*or*	**Whose** are these?	
apple is this?	*or*	apples are these?	

It's	**mine.**	They're	**mine.**
	yours.		**yours.**
	his.		**his.**
	hers.		**hers.**
	ours.		**ours.**
	theirs.		**theirs.**

With a person's name, add **'s**. For example:

Whose lunch is this? Whose cookies are these?
It's John**'s**. They're Mary**'s**.

A. **Fill in the blanks.**

1. Whose milk is ___this___? ___It's___ mine.

2. Whose cherries are _____? _____ yours.

3. Whose lunch _____ this? _____ Marta's.

4. Whose sandwiches _____ these? _____ ours.

5. Whose cheese _____? _____ Sid's.

6. Whose tablecloth _____? _____ mine.

B. **Fill in the blanks with his, hers, or theirs.**

1. That lunch belongs to Felipe. It's _____.

2. Those oranges belong to Mary. They're _____.

3. Those boxes belong to Linda. They're _____.

4. That bag belongs to Han and Lu. It's _____.

Always . . . never

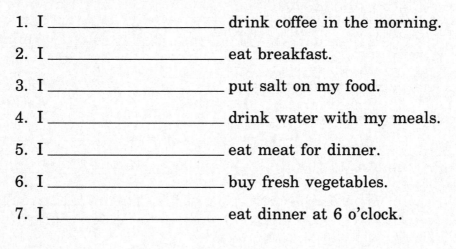

always
usually
often
sometimes
never

I **always** eat eggs for breakfast.
 usually
 often
 sometimes
 never

With *he* and *she*, add **-s** to the action word.

He **usually** eat**s** eggs for breakfast.

A. **Fill in the blanks. Give your own information.**

1. I _____ drink coffee in the morning.

2. I _____ eat breakfast.

3. I _____ put salt on my food.

4. I _____ drink water with my meals.

5. I _____ eat meat for dinner.

6. I _____ buy fresh vegetables.

7. I _____ eat dinner at 6 o'clock.

B. **Fill in the blanks. Give information about a classmate.**

1. He/She _____ drinks juice in the morning.

2. He/She _____ eats breakfast.

3. He/She _____ eats meat for dinner.

4. He/She _____ buys fresh vegetables.

5. He/She _____ eats lunch at noon.

Write It! Say It! Do It!

A. **Look at the picture. What is in the refrigerator?**

<u>radishes</u>   _____

_____   _____

_____   _____

_____   _____

_____   _____

B. **Five people are coming to dinner. You want to make your favorite recipe. What do you need? How much do you need?**
   Work with a classmate. Make a list.

_____   _____

_____   _____

_____   _____

_____   _____

_____   _____

In the future

We often use a form of **be** + verb + **-ing** when we speak of the future.

For example:
I'm **going** downtown tomorrow. My friend **is going** with me.

A. Read the dialogue.

Chico: When **are we going** to buy some new clothes?

Mother: Not tonight. **We're going** to Uncle Paco's house for dinner.

Chico: And tomorrow?

Mother: Tomorrow **you're going** to the dentist.

Chico: But I need new clothes. **I'm starting** school next Monday.

Mother: No. **You're starting** a week from Monday.

Chico: Oh-h-h!

B. Answer the questions.

1. What are Chico and his mother doing tonight?

   _____.

2. What is Chico doing tomorrow?

   _____.

3. What does Chico need?

   _____.

4. Is Chico starting school next Monday?

   _____.

Right now

We also use a form of **be** + verb + **-ing** when we speak of *right now*.
I **am wearing** my new shirt.

What is happening **right now** in the picture? Answer the questions.
Use words from the box.

| dress | shirt | jacket | dolls | ties |

1. What is the man buying?

   He's buying a shirt.

2. What is the little girl looking at?

   _____

3. What is the woman doing?

   _____

4. What is the little boy trying on?

   _____

5. What is the little girl wearing?

   _____

It's usual

We use only the **verb** when we speak of *usual actions.*
I **wear** this shirt every Sunday.

A. Answer the questions. Write complete sentences.

1. What do you usually wear at home?

   _____

2. What do you usually wear to the movies?

   _____

3. Where do you shop for clothes?

   _____

4. Where do you shop for household items?

   _____

5. What size shoes do you wear?

   _____

6. What do you buy on sale?

   _____

B. Ask your classmate the questions in Exercise A. Write his/her answers in complete sentences.

1. _____
2. _____
3. _____
4. _____
5. _____
6. _____

Right now/It's usual

A. Sam is a salesman at Buy-Mart. He is talking to a customer. Complete the dialogue. Use words from the box.

wear	wearing	looking for	prefer

Sam: Good afternoon, sir. May I help you?

Customer: Yes, I'm _____ a new shirt.

Sam: What size shirt do you _____?

Customer: I _____ a 15½ regular.

Sam: What color do you _____?

Customer: I prefer orange—the color I'm

_____ right now. I always

_____ orange.

B. Now Sam is talking to another customer. Complete the dialogue. Use words from the box.

wear	wears	wearing	looking for	prefer

Customer: Hello. I'm _____ a shirt for my husband.

Sam: What size shirt does he _____?

Customer: He _____ a 15½ regular.

Sam: What color does he _____?

Customer: He prefers orange. He always

_____ orange.

Sam: I think I know your husband!

Words that describe things

Words that describe come **after** a form of **be**—
That dress is **beautiful**.

or **before** the thing they describe—
I like that **silk** shirt.

**A. Sylvia and Carmen are talking. Complete their dialogue.
Use words from the box below.**

| big | good | beautiful | black | white | striped | silk |

Sylvia:　My _____ friend Rosa is getting married tomorrow.

Carmen:　What is she wearing?

Sylvia:　She's wearing a _____ _____ dress.

Carmen:　What is the groom wearing?

Sylvia:　He's wearing a _____ _____ tuxedo.

B. Describe what a classmate is wearing right now.

_____

_____

_____

_____

C. Imagine something wonderful. You want to buy it. Describe it.

_____

_____

_____

_____

Write It! Say It! Do It!

A. Imagine that you are at Buy-Mart right now. What are the customers doing? Use words from the box.

looking at	looking for	trying on	buying	asking about

1. A mother and her baby _____.

   _____.

2. Two teen-age boys _____.

   _____.

3. A little girl _____.

   _____.

4. A boy and his grandmother _____.

   _____.

B. Write sentences about your shopping habits.

1. _____.
2. _____.
3. _____.
4. _____.

C. Answer the questions.

1. What are you doing tonight?

   _____.

2. What are you doing this weekend?

   _____.

3. Where are you going on your next vacation?

   _____.

Unit 7

□ **There is/there are**
□ **Some/any**
□ **Persons and things**

There is/there are

To say that something exists, use:

There is *or* **There's** → *one* person or thing

There are → *two or more* persons or things

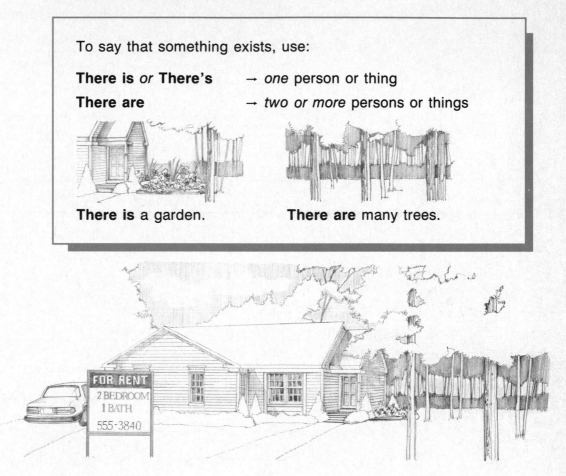

There is a garden. **There are** many trees.

Look at the picture. Fill in the blanks with There is or There are.

1. _____ a sign near the house.

2. _____ two bedrooms in the house.

3. _____ one bathroom.

4. _____ a wide driveway.

5. _____ a large front yard.

6. _____ a lot of flowers in the garden.

7. _____ front steps.

There is/there are: Questions and answers

Questions:	Short answers:
Is there a garage?	Yes, **there is.**
Is there a front porch?	No, **there isn't.**
Are there three bedrooms?	Yes, **there are.**
Are there two bathrooms?	No, **there aren't.**

A. **Emilio and a real estate agent are talking. Fill in the blanks.
Use Is there, Are there, and short answers.**

Emilio: Hello. I have some questions about the house at
345 Maple Street.

Agent: Of course. Please sit down.

Emilio: _____ a lease?

Agent: Yes, _____. _____ a
six-month lease.

Emilio: _____ many children in the neighborhood?

Agent: Yes, _____. _____ a

little boy next door, and _____ two little
girls down the street.

B. **Work with a classmate. Ask and answer questions about each other's
homes.**

For example: two bathrooms in the house

Question: Are there two bathrooms in the house?
Answer: Yes, there are. *or* No, there aren't.

1. large closets in the bedrooms

2. a refrigerator in the kitchen

3. a smoke detector in the house

4. a washing machine in the laundry room

5. a shower in the bathroom

Some/any

Use **some** with the affirmative.

> There *is* **some** space for a washer and dryer.
> There *are* **some** outlets in the kitchen.

Use **any** with the negative.

> There *isn't* **any** space for a washer and dryer.
> There *aren't* **any** outlets in the kitchen.

Use **any** with questions.

> Is there **any** space for a washer and dryer?
> Are there **any** outlets in the kitchen?

A. Fill in the blanks with some or any.

1. "Is there any storage space in the garage?"

   "There isn't _____ storage space in the garage, but

   there is _____ storage space in the basement."

2. "Is there any wallpaper in the house?"

   "There's _____ wallpaper in the living room, but

   there isn't _____ wallpaper in the bedrooms."

3. "Are there any children in the neighborhood?"

   "There aren't _____ children, but there are

   _____ teen-agers across the street."

4. "Are there any closets in the hall?"

   "There aren't _____ closets in the hall, but there are

   _____ large closets in the bedroom."

B. Write about your house or apartment.

1. In my house/apartment, there are some _____.

2. There aren't any _____.

Persons and things

Mommy is watching **me.**   Mommy is watching **you.**

Mrs. Bates is watching John.   She's watching **him.**
                       Cathy.   **her.**
                       a TV program.   **it.**
                       you and me.   **us.**
                       John and Cathy.   **them.**

A. Rewrite these sentences. Change the underlined words. Use him, her, it, us, or them.

1. I know <u>Cathy</u>. I know _____.

2. I know <u>John</u>. I know _____.

3. I know <u>Mr. and Mrs. Bates</u>. I know _____.

4. John knows <u>my wife and me</u>. He knows _____.

5. <u>I</u> know you, and you know _____.

6. I know <u>the neighborhood</u>. I know _____ well.

B. Fill in the blanks. Use you, him, her, it, us.

1. My husband and I need an apartment. Can you help _____?

2. Yes. I can help _____.

3. This is a nice apartment. I like _____.

4. There's a little boy next door. Your son will like _____.

5. Ms. Gomez is the owner. Call _____ in the morning.

Persons and things

Use **me, you, him, her, it, us, them** after words like *at, to, for,* and *with.*

Robert is talking to **me.**   Robert is talking to **us.**
        you.   **them.**
        him.
        her.

A. Fill in the blanks of the dialogue. Use me, you, her, it, us.

Robert: Hi, Peter. I'm going to see an apartment this afternoon.

Can you come with _____ to look at _____?

Peter: Yes. I can come with _____.

Robert: Good. The owner, Mrs. Vega, will meet _____

there. I need to talk to _____.

B. Rewrite these sentences. Change the underlined words. Use him, it, us, them.

Nora calls Mr. Fuentes, her landlord. She says to <u>the landlord</u>, "My kitchen sink is broken. Please fix <u>the kitchen sink</u> right away." The landlord arrives. He talks and plays with Nora's children. He laughs with <u>the children</u>. Nora says, "Please fix the sink! You can talk to <u>the children and me</u> tomorrow."

_____

_____

_____

_____

_____

_____

_____

Write It! Say It! Do It!

A. Sophia is in her garage. She is looking for building materials to make a fence. What does she see? Use **There is some, There are some, There isn't any, There aren't any**.

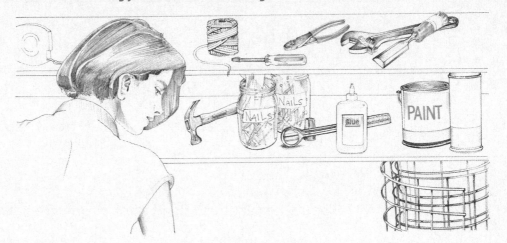

1. _____ nails.

2. _____ glue.

3. _____ chicken wire.

4. _____ lumber.

5. _____ tools.

6. _____ brushes.

7. _____ string.

8. _____ sandpaper.

B. Read the sentences. Fill in the blanks with **it, her, him, them**.

1. There's some paint in the garage. Sophia needs _____.

2. There's some glue on the shelf, but she doesn't need _____.

3. There are some nails on the shelf. She needs _____.

4. Sophia's husband Nick often helps _____.

5. Tomorrow she's helping _____ with the garden.

6. Sometimes Sophia and Nick's neighbors help _____.

□ **Have/has**
□ **Have to/has to**
□ **Would like**
□ **Want/need/like**

Have/has

> To say that something *belongs* to someone, use **have** *or* **has**.
>
> I   **have** a headache.   He   **has** a headache.
> You   She
> We
> They
>
> For the negative, use **don't have** *or* **doesn't have**.
>
> I   **don't have** the flu.   He   **doesn't have** the flu.
> You   She
> We
> They

A. Fill in the blanks with have or has.

Carol and Manuel don't feel well. Carol _____ a

runny nose. Manuel _____ itchy eyes. They both

_____ appointments this morning to see the doctor.

Carol _____ an appointment at 10:30, and Manuel

_____ one at 11:00.

B. Fill in the blanks with don't have or doesn't have.

Fortunately, Carol and Manuel _____ _____

the flu. Carol _____ _____ itchy eyes.

Manuel _____ _____ a runny nose.

However, the doctor says they *both* have allergies.

Have/has: Questions and answers

Question: Answer:

Do you have medical insurance?   Yes, **I**   **do.** *or* No, **I**   **don't.**
  we   **we**   **we**
  they   **they**   **they**

Does she have a sore throat?   Yes, **she does.** *or* No, **she doesn't.**

A. Answer the questions.

1. Do you have a regular doctor? _____.

2. Do you have medical insurance? _____.

3. Do you have a headache right now? _____.

4. Do you have headaches often? _____.

5. Do you have normal blood pressure? _____.

6. Does your classmate have a cough today? _____.

7. Do you have a regular dentist? _____.

8. Do you have a thermometer at home? _____.

B. Look at the pictures. Answer the questions.

1. Does he have a headache?

_____.

2. Does she have a toothache?

_____.

3. Does he have a stomachache?

_____.

4. Does she have a backache?

_____.

Have to/has to

Have to or **has to** $\longrightarrow$ It is *necessary* to do something.

I **have to** take medicine.	He **has to** take medicine.
You	She
We	
They	

A. **What do these people have to do? Write the correct letters.**

_____ 1. I have a cough.

_____ 2. Paco is at the doctor's office. The doctor is with another patient.

_____ 3. You have an appointment with your doctor, but you can't go.

_____ 4. Alicia feels sick.

_____ 5. We want to stay healthy.

a. We have to eat good food.

b. You have to cancel your appointment.

c. She has to stay in bed.

d. I have to take cough medicine.

e. He has to wait.

take aspirin   call the dentist   sit down   stay in bed   call 911

B. **What do you have to do? Write complete sentences. Use words from the box above.**

1. You have a high fever. _____.

2. You see a bad accident. _____.

3. You feel dizzy. _____.

4. You have a toothache. _____

_____.

5. You have the flu. _____

_____.

Would like

To be polite or formal, use **would like** to mean *want*. For example:

I *want* a cough drop.   I **would like** a cough drop.

The short form of **would like** is *person* + **'d like.**

I'd   like a cough drop.   **We'd**   like a cough drop.
You'd   **They'd**
He'd
She'd

A. **Rewrite the sentences. Make them more polite or formal.
Use would like.**

1. I want a glass of water. _____.

2. She wants an aspirin. _____.

3. I want a Band-Aid. _____.

4. He wants some soup. _____.

Question:		Answer:			
Would you like some soup?		Yes, **I**	**would.** *or*	No, **I**	**wouldn't.**
he		he		he	
she		she		she	

B. **Rewrite the questions. Make them more polite or formal.
Use would like.**

1. Do you want some cough medicine?

   _____?

2. Does she want an aspirin?

   _____?

3. Does he want some water?

   _____?

4. Do you want a blanket?

   _____?

Want/need/like

> The *name of a person* or *thing* often follows the words **want**, **need**, or **like**.
> For example:
>
> I **want** *some soup.*   I **need** *an aspirin.*   I **like** *my doctor.*
>
> Sometimes *an action word* follows **want**, **need**, or **like**.
> Use **to** before the action word.
>
> I **want** *to make* an appointment.   I **need** *to go* to the clinic.
>   I **like** *to be* on time.

A. Fill in the blanks with **to get, to see, to take, to exercise, to do, to swim.**

1. Yoko needs _____ her doctor.

2. She wants _____ a check-up.

3. The doctor says, "I need _____ your blood pressure."

4. The doctor says, "You need _____."

5. Yoko says, "I like _____."

6. The doctor says, "Then you need _____ it."

B. Write complete sentences.

1. Name something you like to do.

_____.

2. Name something you need to do today.

_____.

3. Name something you want to do this weekend.

_____.

Write It! Say It! Do It!

A. Imagine that this is a shelf in your bathroom. Fill in the blanks with have and don't have.

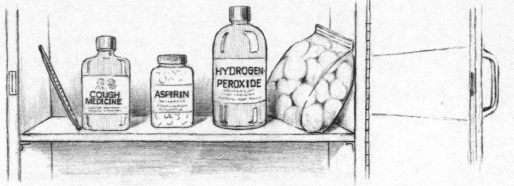

1. I _____ a thermometer, but I _____ any alcohol.

2. I _____ a bottle of aspirin, but I _____ any Band-Aids.

3. I _____ some cotton balls, but I _____ any bandages.

4. I _____ any alcohol, but I _____ some hydrogen peroxide.

5. I _____ any antacid tablets, but I _____ some cough medicine.

B. Imagine that you are sick. Fill in the blanks.

1. I have a _____.

2. I don't have a _____.

3. I'd like a _____.

4. I want to _____.

5. I need some _____.

6. I need to take _____.

7. I don't want any _____.

8. I don't want to _____.

□ Can/can't
□ Past: -ed/-d

Can/can't

can = to be *able* to do something

Affirmative:	Negative:
I **can** type.	I **can't (cannot)** type.
You	You
He	He
She	She
We	We
They	They

A. Tell what these people can do. Use words from the box below.

prepare	make	fix	teach

1. Joan is a carpenter. ___She can make___ furniture.

2. Alan is a mechanic. _____ cars.

3. Bob and Sally are chefs. _____ good food.

4. We're language teachers. _____ English.

B. Tell what these people can't do. Use words from the box below.

fix	open	build	write

1. Joan doesn't have any nails. _____ the shelves.

2. Alan doesn't have his tools. _____ the car.

3. They don't have the keys to the restaurant. _____

   _____ the door.

4. We don't have any chalk. _____ on the board.

Can: Questions and answers

Question: Answer:
Can you drive a truck?   Yes, I **can.**   *or*   No, I **can't.**
Can he type 50 words a minute? Yes, he **can.**   *or*   No, he **can't.**

A. Change the sentences into questions with **can.**

1. She can work part-time.

   _____?

2. Manuel and Sandra can type.

   _____?

3. You can write poetry.

   _____?

4. Rita can repair appliances.

   _____?

5. Tony can wait on tables.

   _____?

B. What can you do? Answer the questions with **Yes, I can** or **No, I can't.**

1. Can you type? _____.

2. Can you cook? _____.

3. Can you use a computer? _____.

4. Can you drive a truck? _____.

5. Can you fix plumbing? _____.

6. Can you speak Spanish? _____.

7. Can you play a musical instrument? _____.

8. Can you draw? _____.

Past: -ed/-d

> To talk about the **past**, we usually add **-ed** or **-d** to the base form of the verb.
>
> For example:
> look → look**ed**   call → call**ed**   save → save**d**   want → want**ed**
>
> I   work**ed** in a hotel last year.   We   work**ed** in a hotel last year.
> You
> He   They

Fill in the blanks. Use verbs from the box below.

worked	cleaned	cleared	washed	cooked	looked after

Last year Eva _worked_

in someone's house. She _____

the house and _____ the meals.

She also _____ the

children. She worked hard.

Eva's husband Jack _____ in

a restaurant. Every day he _____

the tables and _____ the

dishes. He worked hard, too.

Things were very different at home.

Jack _____ the house

and _____ the meals. He also

_____ the children.

Eva _____ the table

and _____ the dishes.

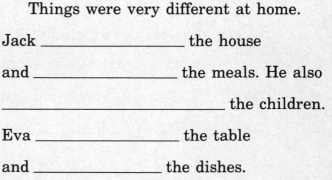

Past: Negatives

To talk about the negative past, we use **did not** or **didn't** + the *base form of the verb.*

Note: With **did not** or **didn't,** the *verb* is in the *present form.*

I **didn't work** last year.
You **didn't wash** the dishes this morning.
He **didn't fix** the car yesterday.

A. **Fill in the blanks. Use didn't + the verb in the present form.**

David lives by himself. Last weekend he tried to do too many things. He didn't finish all his work.

He washed the plates, but he ___didn't wash___ the windows. He cleaned the kitchen, but he

_____ his car. He waxed the table, but he

_____ the floor. He fixed a broken water pipe,

but he _____ the leaking roof. He painted the

kitchen ceiling, but he _____ the kitchen

walls. He watered the grass, but he _____ the garden.

B. **Fill in the blanks. Use didn't + one of the following verbs: have, like, get, see.**

Rosa _____ a good day yesterday. She parked

her car near the bank, but she _____ the "No Parking" sign. At work, she received her pay check, but she

_____ the right amount. She ordered food in

a restaurant, but she _____ what she ordered.
Poor Rosa!

Past: Questions and answers

Question:		Answer:				
Did you	answer the ad?	Yes, **I**	**did.**	*or*	No, **I**	**didn't.**
he		**he**		*or*	**he**	
we		**we**		*or*	**we**	
they		**they**		*or*	**they**	

A. Change these sentences into questions.

1. He started a new job last month.

   _____?

2. She worked in a grocery store three years ago.

   _____?

3. They stocked the shelves in the store last night.

   _____?

4. Harry moved to another department in the company.

   _____?

B. Look at the pictures. Then answer the questions.

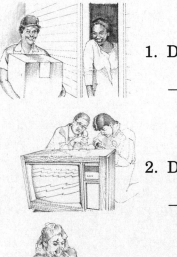

1. Did he deliver a package?

   _____.

2. Did they repair the TV?

   _____.

3. Did she drop the food?

   _____.

Write It! Say It! Do It!

A. Write did you in the blanks to make questions. Then ask a classmate these questions.

1. _____ work in your country?

2. Where _____ work?

3. _____ work on weekends?

4. What _____ do?

5. How long _____ have that job?

B. Write your classmate's answers below.

1. _____.

2. _____.

3. _____.

4. _____.

5. _____.

C. Write complete sentences.

1. Name two things you liked about a job in your past.

   _____.

   _____.

2. Name two things you didn't like about a job in your past.

   _____.

   _____.

3. When you were a child, what person did you admire?
   Describe that person's job.

   _____

   _____

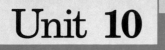

Unit 10

- □ **Was/were**
- □ **Wasn't/weren't**
- □ **Why . . . ?**

Was/were

The past of **be:**

Persons

I was happy.   **We were** happy.
You were
He was   **They were**
She was

Things

The food **was** delicious.   The beaches **were** beautiful.
It was delicious.   **They were** beautiful.

Fill in the blanks with **was** or **were**.

1. Last week I _____ in Miami.

2. The weather _____ beautiful.

3. The beaches _____ wonderful.

4. My hotel room _____ nice.

5. The people _____ friendly.

6. The food _____ delicious.

7. The flight _____ perfect.

8. It _____ a great trip.

9. I _____ in heaven!

Was/were: Negatives

Negative past → Add **not** after **was** or **were**.

Persons

I was not   here last week.   **We were not**   here last week.
He was not   **You were not**
She was not   **They were not**

A. Everyone was out of town last week. Where were they?
Fill in the blanks. Use **was not** or **were not**.

1. I _____ _____ here. I was in Palm Springs.

2. You _____ _____ here. You were in Anaheim.

3. Jack _____ _____ here. He was in San Diego.

4. Mary _____ _____ here. She was in Los Angeles.

5. Bob and Susan _____ _____ here. They were in
Pasadena.

Things

The trip was cheap.   The beaches were empty.
It was not expensive.   **They were not** crowded.

B. Rewrite these sentences. Make them negative. Use **was not** or
were not.

1. The trip was enjoyable.

   _____

2. The hotel was large.

   _____

3. The beaches were clean.

   _____

4. The weather was very hot.

   _____

Was/were: Negatives

The short form of *was not* → **wasn't**
The short form of *were not* → **weren't**

A. **Read about Phillip's vacation. Fill in the blanks.**
   Use wasn't or weren't.

Last week Phillip traveled by bus with some friends. It

_____ a good trip. The bus _____ very

comfortable. The hotel rooms _____ clean. Phillip and

his friends wanted to swim, but the hotel _____ near

the beach. They walked and walked to get to the beach. When

they finally arrived there, the beach _____ clean. The

water _____ clean, either. Phillip and his friends

_____ very happy.

B. **Now Phillip is home. He is writing a letter to his brother Dimitri. Fill in**
   the blanks. Use the past of be: was, wasn't, were, or weren't.

Dear Dimitri,
   I went to the coast last week with some
friends. We traveled by bus. It _____ crowded
on the bus and we _____ very comfortable.
When we arrived at our hotel, we _____
really tired. The rooms weren't cheap and
they _____ very clean, either.
   It _____ a hot day, so we decided to go
to the beach. The hotel _____ very close to
the beach, so we walked for a long time.
When we arrived there, the beach _____ filthy
and the water _____ polluted.
   What a vacation! I'm glad to be home!
   Your brother,
                    Phillip

Was/were: Questions and answers

Persons

Question: Answer:
Was he   on a trip last week? Yes, **he was.**   *or* No, **he wasn't.**
Were they   Yes, **they were.** *or* No, **they weren't.**

Things

Question: Answer:
Was the weather nice?
Was it nice?   Yes, **it was.**   *or* No, **it wasn't.**

Were the tickets expensive?
Were they expensive?   Yes, **they were.** *or* No, **they weren't.**

**Interview a classmate. Ask about a trip he/she took as a child. Or ask him/her to imagine such a trip. Write your classmate's answers.
Use complete sentences.**

1. Were you alone on your trip? _____

   _____.

2. Was the weather nice? _____

   _____.

3. Was it a long trip? _____

   _____.

4. Was the food good? _____

   _____.

5. Were you in a hotel? _____

   _____.

6. Were you glad to return home? _____

   _____.

Why . . . ?

Underline one of the words in parentheses. Fill in the blank with the word (or words) you underlined. Then answer the questions.

1. Why are you (happy, sad) right now? I am _____ because

   _____ .

2. Why do you usually (take the bus, walk, drive) to class? I usually

   _____ to class because _____

   _____ .

3. Why are you (moving to another town, staying in the same town)

   next year? _____

   _____ because _____

   _____ .

4. Why did you move to the U. S. (recently, a long time ago)? I moved

   to the U. S. _____ because _____

   _____

   _____ .

5. Why were you (on time, late) for class today? I was _____

   for class today because _____

   _____

   _____ .

Write It! Say It! Do It!

A. Imagine that you took a dream vacation. Where did you go? Look for a picture in a magazine or travel brochure of that place. Paste it below. Tell about your imaginary trip. Use **was, wasn't, were,** or **weren't.**

I traveled to _____.

I _____ there for _____ weeks.

I traveled by _____. I _____

comfortable on the _____. The _____

_____ expensive. The weather _____

_____ and _____. I _____ happy

to return home.

B. Answer questions about your imaginary trip.

1. Was it an unusual trip?

_____.

2. Was it an expensive trip?

_____.

3. Was the weather nice?

_____.

4. Were the people friendly?

_____.

5. Was the food good?

_____.